BODY TALK

SMELL, TASTE AND TOUCH

THE SENSORY SYSTEMS

JENNY BRYAN

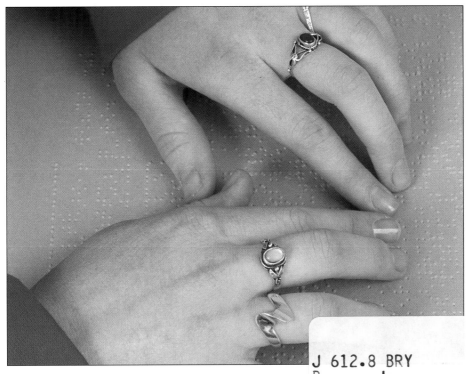

Dillon Press
New York

BODY TALK

BREATHING

DIGESTION

MIND AND MATTER

MOVEMENT

REPRODUCTION

SMELL, TASTE AND TOUCH

SOUND AND VISION

THE PULSE OF LIFE

First Dillon Press Edition 1994

Dillon Press
Macmillan Publishing Company
866 Third Avenue
New York, NY 10022

Macmillan Publishing Company is part of the Maxwell Communication Group of Companies.

First published in 1993 by Wayland (Publishers) Limited
61 Western Road, Hove, East Sussex, England BN3 1JD

Library of Congress Cataloging-in-Publication Data

Bryan, Jenny,
        Smell, taste and touch : the sensory systems/Jenny Bryan.—1st
Dillon Press ed.
   p.   cm. — (Body talk)
   Includes index.
   ISBN: 0-87518-590-8
   1. Smell—Juvenile literature. 2. Taste—Juvenile literature. 3.
Touch—Juvenile literature. [1. Smell. 2. Taste. 3. Touch. 4. Senses
and sensation.] I. Title. II. Series.
QP458.B79 1994
612.8—dc20   93-36759

Summary: Describes the senses of smell, taste and touch and
explores the ways these senses affect our lives.

Printed by G. Canale & C.S.p.A., Turin, Italy

1 2 3 4 5 6 7 8 9 10

CONTENTS

INTRODUCTION

You only have to watch a dog on the scent of a rabbit to know that humans have a relatively undeveloped sense of smell. We couldn't smell a rabbit if it was right under our noses. In the same way, insects have a more highly developed sense of taste than us. When you see a bee lapping up the nectar from a flower, you know it's on to a good thing. Insects can taste sugar in liquids at concentrations over 1,000 times less than we would need to find something sweet.

In fact, the human body is inferior to others in the animal kingdom in almost every way. The big cats can move faster, and bats can hear better. Without our superior brains, we would definitely be at the bottom of the pile!

However, we have learned to use the special senses of other animals to make up for our own shortcomings. Dogs help people with poor eyesight and hearing. More recently, they have been trained to sniff out drugs and explosives. But we still need human guinea pigs to try new flavors in our food. We can't yet rely on bluebottle flies to tell us what tastes good!

Touch is our most personal sense. Some people use it more than others. Whether it is a hug or just a light brush on the arm, touch can tell us more about what a person is thinking than hundreds of words. Think about the different signals you give off. If we use them well, our senses can bring us a lot of pleasure.

LEFT Insects have a more developed sense of taste than humans.

RIGHT This grandfather and grandson don't need words to tell each other how they feel. A hug says it all.

SMELL IT OR TASTE IT?

When you take a mouthful of food, your brain is bombarded with messages from your nose and mouth. Your eyes also send information about what your food looks like and your memory tells you how something on your plate should smell and taste. You'd get quite a shock if something that looked like a piece of meat tasted of rhubarb and custard and smelled like brussels sprouts!

High up in your nose, hairlike cells in the lining detect smells as they waft past. The cells then send signals along nerves to the olfactory bulb—the receiving center near the front of the brain where smell signals are interpreted.

It's a tricky job. The human nose is very sensitive and can distinguish among some 10,000 different smells. Your nose needs to be able to distinguish among the smell of what you are eating and background smells coming from other people's meals, the kitchen, the street, and numerous other places. Sometimes a smell nearby is so strong that your nose can't concentrate on anything else. But in that case your tongue will help you out.

RIGHT You probably wouldn't be able to smell the strawberries if you stood near this table. The smell of the food in the casserole would be much more powerful.

6

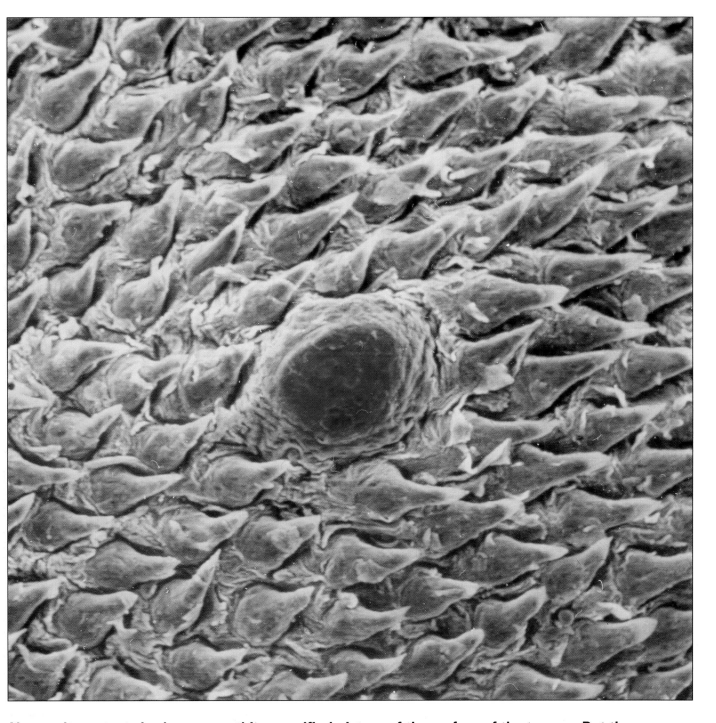

You can't see taste buds even on this magnified picture of the surface of the tongue. But they are found on top of these conelike structures.

Taste is detected at thousands of sites on the tongue, called taste buds. Again, hairlike cells reach up from the surface of the tongue to sample the foods passing by. They relay the information back to goblet-shaped cells in the tongue that, in turn, send information along nerves to the taste zone of the brain.

Taste buds are not all-purpose. Some respond to sweet tastes, some to sour, some to salty, and some to bitter tastes. The sweet area is at the front of the tongue, and the salty area is just behind it on either side. Running down most of each side of the tongue is the sour zone. The bitter zone is along the back of the tongue.

FAILED SENSES

If you want to lose your senses of taste and smell, the best thing you can do is take up smoking. The chemicals in tobacco keep the taste and smell cells in the tongue and nose from working properly. The result is that everything smells and tastes much the same. No more delicious-tasting chocolate, salty sea air, or freshly mown grass smells!

NICE SMELLS, BAD SMELLS

What's your favorite smell? Roast beef in the oven? Freshly washed clothes? Spring flowers? Rain? We all have different ideas about what smells good. But we know what smells bad—manure, rotting vegetables, milk that's spoiled, a dead rat.

Why don't we like these smells? It isn't our noses that tell us when something smells good or bad. They just report what they've found. It's the way our brains interpret the information arriving from our noses that determines whether we like or dislike a particular smell.

From a very early age we link certain smells with what we see. We watch our parents turn their noses up at the smell of manure and so we do the same. We see what makes the smell and remember that it's unpleasant the next time we see or smell it. We see someone smile as they smell flowers or sniff the Sunday dinner and we know that these are good smells.

These young people will probably always think of happy summer days when they smell grassy meadows.

We learn that milk tastes sour when it is spoiled, and we learn to link the smell of sour milk with the fact that it doesn't taste nice. So our noses act as early warning systems and keep us from drinking something unpleasant.

Sometimes our nasal early warning systems save us from more dangerous situations. We cannot see or hear gas, but we can smell it and we know that it can kill us. Similarly, we can smell something burning long before we see flames or hear the crackle of a fire.

With luck, you won't smell a dead rat very often! But even before you learn to link the smell with the rotting body, you'll know that this is quite different from anything else you've smelled before. Your memory will tell you that this isn't manure or rotting cabbage or sour milk, but something even more unpleasant.

Some people claim that they can smell some rather surprising things, such as a storm coming or a fight about to happen. It is possible to smell fear because people tend to sweat when they are frightened.

RIGHT Some people claim they can smell a storm coming. Can you?

BODY ODOR

Children's sweat has very little smell. But after puberty, if sweat remains on the skin for long, bacteria gets into it and starts to break it down. That's when it starts to smell. You can prevent body odor by washing regularly, especially under your arms, so that sweat does not build up on your body. You can then use deodorants and antiperspirants to make your skin smell nicer and reduce the amount of sweat getting onto your skin. Some people have body odor even though they wash every day. This is because they do not change their clothes often enough. Sweat gets into clothes and the smell stays until it is washed out.

SEXY SMELLS

A female silk moth can attract male moths from miles around by releasing a chemical into the air called a pheromone. Most female animals release similar chemicals when they are ready to mate. You only have to watch a pack of male dogs following a female in heat to guess just how strong these pheromones must be.

Humans appear to have lost the ability to detect pheromones, which may be just as well! But it hasn't stopped people from looking for them and even selling them.

Some people do seem to have a particular "smell." But this may be more to do with their washing habits—or lack of them—than anything else. They simply may have body odors. Scientists have isolated minute quantities of certain steroids, that could be sexual attractants, from secretions released from human armpits. One has been likened to the finest quality sandalwood, another to a cross between smelly old socks and pigs! The problem is that most people cannot smell them at all.

This female silk moth is leaving sexy messages for her partner.

Why have humans lost their abilities to release and to detect pheromones? One reason may be that we no longer need them. Many animals, such as tigers and leopards, live most of their lives alone and only come together to mate. Others, such as elephants, live in groups of separate sexes. The males need to know when to visit the local females.

Human culture is much more closely knit. The sexes mix daily, not just to mate and reproduce. We have also developed language as a method of communicating our needs to one another. And, even if we did produce pheromones, they'd be pretty hard to detect against the wall of soaps, cosmetics, and perfumes with which we assault each other.

WHAT A SMELL!

Some animals use smell as a defense mechanism. The best known is probably the skunk. When it gets angry or frightened, it releases a foul-smelling chemical.

BELOW Pheromones probably haven't had much to do with what these people think of each other.

PERFUMES

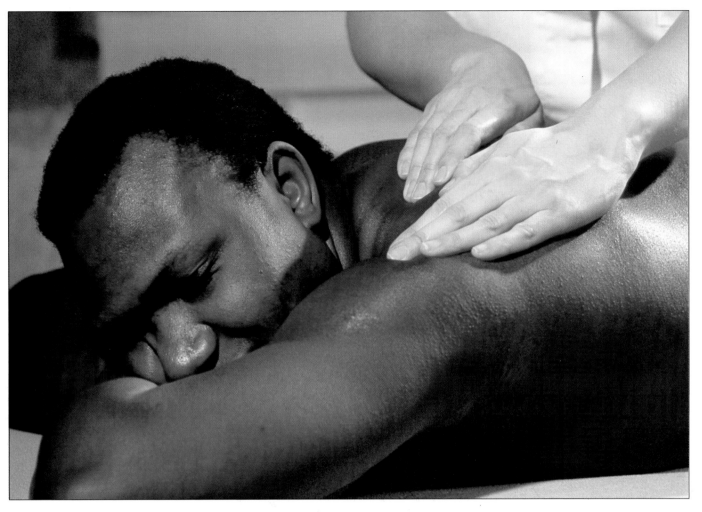

Enjoying aromatherapy doesn't mean you're a wimp! It can help anyone relax.

"Wear Chanel No. 5 whenever you expect to be kissed" was the advice of the legendary designer Coco Chanel. You may not be able to afford Chanel No. 5, but whatever perfume or aftershave a man or woman chooses, they are telling those around them something about themselves and how they are feeling.

If you choose a bold, powerful fragrance, you are announcing that you can take on the world. You are feeling outgoing and fiery and you want everyone to know about it. If you choose something lighter, more subtle, it doesn't mean you're a wimp. You just go about things more quietly, less openly. You may be feeling thoughtful and at peace with yourself and the world. People know you are there, so you don't need to shout it from the rooftops.

At one time, men and women stuck to one aftershave or perfume and wore it all the time. Today, many people have several and wear what goes with their mood, their clothes, and what they are planning to do.

Most perfumes are musk- or flower-based. Musk is the heavy scent produced by many male animals, notably the musk deer, and it is considered to be a sexual attractant. You might wear a musky perfume in the evening and a lighter, floral perfume during the day.

Some perfumes smell differently on different people because they combine with the natural oils in the skin. So it is important to try a perfume or aftershave on your skin before buying it.

Many people believe that particular smells have healing properties. They use aromatherapy oils to cheer them up when they are feeling low or calm them down when they are feeling anxious. Aromatherapy oils—made from plants—can be dissolved in the bath or diluted and massaged into the skin. Certainly, if you put lavender, lemon, or pine oil in the bath, you'll feel refreshed. Eucalyptus oil will clear your head, and rose, cedarwood, or cypress oil will make you relaxed and sleepy. But no one has proved scientifically that oils can cure diseases.

SPLASH IT ON ALL OVER

Twenty years ago, British boxer Henry Cooper urged men to splash Brut aftershave on all over. Millions of bottles were sold. Today, men have a much wider choice of aftershaves and competition is tough. So the manufacturers of Brut take a more subtle approach.

Henry Cooper was good for the Brut tough, macho image when he was a top boxer. But today the manufacturers go for a softer image.

FLAVOR

It's a dog's life! It doesn't look as if there'll be any left over for the spaniel.

You wouldn't eat roast beef with ice cream, or lamb with chocolate mousse, would you? But you'd probably happily wolf down chicken in a cream sauce. Each combination is mixing meat with a soft, sweeter dairy product. The last one works, but most people would find the first two combinations horrible.

The mixtures of food that we eat have evolved over thousands of years. Prehistoric humans wouldn't have taken kindly to cooking their meat, let alone covering it with a rich, creamy sauce! Medieval humans would have thought nothing of consuming course after course of different roasted meats with hardly a vegetable in sight. And Victorian households would have been pretty unenthusiastic about being served a salad for dinner.

So what makes a meal appetizing to twentieth-century humans? We want a mixture of colors, textures, and flavors on our plates. Whether we are meat eaters or vegetarians, most of us want something fairly solid that we can get our teeth into—a lamb chop, some crisp vegetables, or a piece of fruit, perhaps. Then we want a mixture of flavors, some strong and some light, some sweet and some sour.

Young people tend to have a sweeter tooth than older people. As you get older, you will probably find that you start to prefer spicy things to very sweet things. Some people like heavily seasoned food and put a lot of salt on their meals. This is bad for their health and it often spoils the natural flavor of their food.

If all the food on your plate is highly flavored, your taste buds get confused because everything takes on the flavor of the strongest item. This is what happens when you have a very hot curry or chili.

But you don't want your food to be too bland. A whole plate of mashed potatoes or rice is rather dull. Some foods bring out the flavor of others. Just think how different a duck tastes, for example, with an orange or plum sauce, than when it is served alone. Or how a sprig of mint can liven up a bowl of peas.

Bad restaurants use sauces to cover up their mistakes. Poor cuts of meat or dishes that are badly prepared are served up awash with sauces in the hope that it will make them taste better. Of course, it doesn't!

Put more than one or two of these peppers into food, and you won't be able to taste any of the other ingredients.

FOOD FADS

An ice-cream and peanut butter sandwich may sound horrible to you. But it could be bliss to a pregnant woman. Some women do have cravings for odd combinations of foods while they are pregnant, but it's less common than you might think.

CHANGING TASTES

Arranging a few lettuce leaves and a piece of tomato on a plate has been turned into a work of art. Unlike anything else you buy, it is often the case that the more you pay for a meal in a restaurant, the less food you get! Pay $4 at a fast-food restaurant and your plate will be laden with food. Sign a credit card slip for $50 a person at a top restaurant and you could go home hungry! Fifteen years ago, to go in search of "nouvelle cuisine" meant you were looking for new, exciting recipes. Today, it implies you are planning to have a small meal on a large plate.

ABOVE This nouvelle cuisine dish probably cost more than a three-course meal for two in a moderately priced restaurant.

OPPOSITE Just a few of the many herbs and spices we use to flavor our food.

Tastes in food have changed dramatically since World War II. When rationing finally ended, people were eager to make up for the years of doing without. No family Sunday was complete without a roast and at least two vegetables, usually followed by a pie or cake that would be guaranteed to leave everyone snoozing in their armchairs for the rest of the afternoon. The better off you were, the more often you had meat and rich, sweet luxury goods, such as bakery cakes and cookies. Those with less money filled up with "stodgy" foods such as potatoes and dumplings.

Now all that has changed. Few people eat meat every day; many choose fish or white meat instead of beef or lamb—not because they cannot afford expensive beef but because they feel that fish and chicken are better for them. In fact, many types of fish you find in stores cost much more than beef. Thousands of people have given up meat and fish altogether.

Travel abroad has introduced millions of people to foreign food. When your grandparents were children, they were unlikely to have had pasta and rice in the cupboard. "Seasoning" food meant adding salt and pepper, not the huge range of herbs and spices available today. Just count how many foreign foods there are in your kitchen and the wide range of countries they come from.

SCHOOL LUNCHES

What are your school lunches like? Most schools now offer a choice of dishes, reflecting changing opinions on what is healthy. This means less fried food and fewer sugary foods and more fresh fruit and vegetables.

MAKING A NEW CHOCOLATE BAR

What's your favorite chocolate bar? Mars? Hershey's? Snickers? There are about 6,000 different kinds of candies to tempt you into parting with your hard-earned money. Seven out of ten have chocolate in them. But big manufacturers such as Mars and Hershey's are always looking for new best-sellers.

Tastes change; one year people want more nuts in their chocolate bars, another year they want more fudge, cookies, or raisins. Manufacturers have got to react quickly to changing demands or their customers will switch to rival brands.

Before a company makes a new chocolate bar, it does a lot of research. First, it asks its customers what they would like. But who should it ask? An eleven-year-old boy will want a very different chocolate bar from a seventy-year-old woman. So a company must decide what age group it is going to target with its new product.

Having found out what its customers want in their chocolate bar, the manufacturer needs to ask a few more questions. When and where are you going to eat it? Are you going to eat it on its own or with something else? What will you be doing while you are eating it?

Can you guess why the company needs to ask these questions? The sort of bar you will buy as a snack to keep you going between meals will be much smaller and lighter than a high-calorie bar you would eat instead of a meal. A snack you are going to eat alone can be a single item. But if you are likely to eat it with friends, you may want to offer them some of it. So you must be able to break it into pieces. If you are eating a snack on its own, it will need to be quite moist. But if the manufacturers expect you to eat it with a drink, they can make it drier.

Which would you prefer? Large or small, hard center or soft? Milk, dark, or white chocolate?

Chocoholics are people who eat more than twelve bars of chocolate a week. How much chocolate do you eat?

Mess is another important factor. If you are at the movies and you want a snack, you don't want it to make lots of crumbs all over your clothes and the seat. You want something you can bite into or chew. But if you are sitting at a table with a plate, it doesn't matter if there are crumbs. So your snack can be drier and more crumbly.

Having decided what you want in your chocolate bar and when you are going to eat it, the chocolate company will then try to make it. The company must make something different enough to stand out from the crowd. But it mustn't be too different or people may not like it.

When the company has a prototype, it can test the new chocolate bar on potential customers. And only if the manufacturer is quite sure it's a hit will the company start to produce it in large quantities and advertise it.

CHOCOHOLICS

Most people love chocolate from the moment they taste it for the first time. On average we eat four bars per week. An average chocoholic will eat twelve and a half, and some eat an incredible seventy bars a week. Eight out of ten chocoholics feel guilty about their addiction and wish they could stop.

BLOODSUCKERS

What do leeches, mosquitoes, and Count Dracula have in common? They all have a taste for blood.

Drop a leech onto your skin and, unless it is already bloated with blood, it will instantly sink powerful suckers at either end of its wormlike body into your flesh. At the same time, it will secrete a powerful chemical, called an anti-coagulant, onto your skin to stop your blood from clotting. Thoughtfully, it will also inject some anesthetic so it doesn't hurt you as it sucks your blood. Only when it has drunk its fill of blood and it is bloated to several times its normal size will it pull out its suckers and drop to the ground.

For centuries, leeches were commonly used in medicine. If in doubt, the doctor would routinely "bleed" his or her patients with leeches to get rid of whatever was wrong with them. Often, "bleeding" was the last thing the patients needed. Already weak from their illness, the loss of blood made them worse than ever.

Leeches are still used in medicine, but only when the patient definitely has too much blood! For example, in plastic surgery it takes time for a skin graft to set up its own blood supply. Blood may be able to get in but not out. If it builds up, the new tissue may be hopelessly damaged. Leeches several inches long are sometimes used to suck out the excess blood.

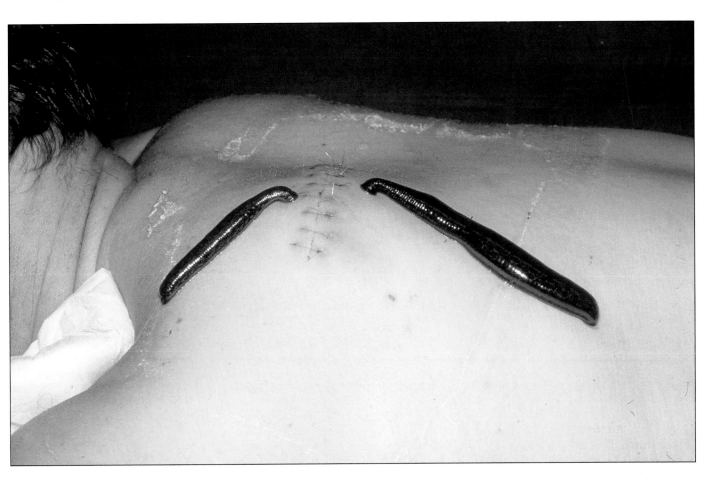

These leeches are doing this man a lot of good, getting rid of excess blood near his scar. But it's probably better that he can't see them.

Leeches, unlike mosquitoes, do not carry diseases. The mosquito's taste for blood causes millions of deaths a year from malaria. Mosquitoes carrying the malaria parasite pass on the infection to people they bite. Even with modern drugs, some strains of malaria parasite can prove fatal. If you go to a place where malaria is common, such as Africa, Southeast Asia, and South America, it is very important to use antimosquito sprays to avoid getting bitten and to take special drugs to prevent malaria in case a mosquito does bite you.

Count Dracula was a figment of author Bram Stoker's vivid imagination. Most types of bats eat fruit, insects, or fish. But some species living in the tropics do survive solely on blood. They make a small cut with their teeth and lap, rather than suck, the blood from their victims, which have, on rare occasions, included sleeping humans. But they don't drink enough to kill and their victims do not turn into bats! However, bats do transmit diseases such as rabies.

Christopher Lee as Count Dracula sinks his teeth into Isla Blair playing Lucy Paxton, one of the characters in the 1969 film *Taste the Blood of Dracula*.

MAN-EATER

When a mentally unstable young man jumped into a lion's cage at the London Zoo in 1992, he was badly mauled. The lion did what any big cat would do if threatened: It attacked. In the wild, lions, tigers, leopards, and cheetahs tend to avoid humans. Only if they are old or injured and cannot catch their usual prey will they turn to catching domestic animals and even humans. Man-eaters are usually hunted down and killed, not because they have got a "taste" for humans, but because, having found out how easy it is to kill one for dinner, they will go on doing it.

IN GOOD TASTE

When American comedy actor Roseanne Arnold sang the national anthem off-key to an audience of thousands, her performance was panned. People asked how any loyal American citizen could do something in such poor taste.

Taste doesn't just refer to what you put in your mouth. Taste has come to mean much more than that. For example, we have taste in music, taste in books, taste in clothes, and taste in household furnishings.

Just because something is not to your taste doesn't mean that it is wrong or bad. You may have a taste for computer games and rap music; your parents may prefer watching TV and listening to rock music. Your tastes are different. It would be arrogant to say you had "better taste" than they do!

Something is usually described as in poor taste when it is offensive to other people. Many comedians tread a fine line between being very funny and being offensive. How do politicians feel when they see themselves made fun of on a television program? We may find it very funny, but what do they and their families think about it?

To have good taste in clothes is now more important than ever before. Some brands of clothes are seen to be in better taste than others. Your sneakers must be Nike, your jeans Calvin Klein. These labels are a lot more expensive than other brands, and they may not be any better.

Is it a good thing that we have become so taste conscious? Do you judge your friends by the clothes they wear or by what they are like? Should we choose our politicians by how they look on television or by what they stand for?

Like it or not, appearances do count. If you go to an interview wearing dirty clothes, you probably won't get the job. But you shouldn't be turned down just because you aren't wearing an Armani suit!

Is having good taste in clothes a matter of wearing what's in fashion, or does it depend on what suits you?

MADONNA

Her records top the charts, her concerts are a sellout, her book was a best-seller. But Madonna is always out to shock. Does she have a real talent or will she do anything for the money? What sort of taste does she have —good or bad?

TOUCH

Press your finger as hard as you can against your desk without hurting yourself. Now rest your finger on your desk as lightly as you can, so it's barely touching it. Whether you press hard or softly, your finger is still sending messages to your brain that it is touching the desk.

In the outer layer of the skin, called the epidermis, are thousands of nerve endings that are sensitive to the smallest changes in pressure on the skin. They are called touch receptors. They can detect a feather brushing across your face, a draft of air behind your neck, or a drop of water on your foot. Their job is to send messages back to the large nerves in your spinal cord, which in turn send messages to your brain.

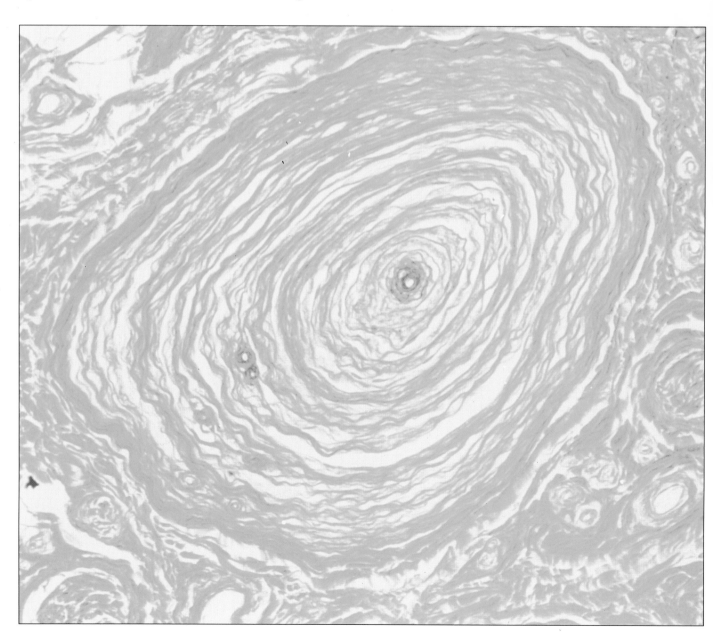

This touch receptor can register changes in pressure on the skin. False color has been added.

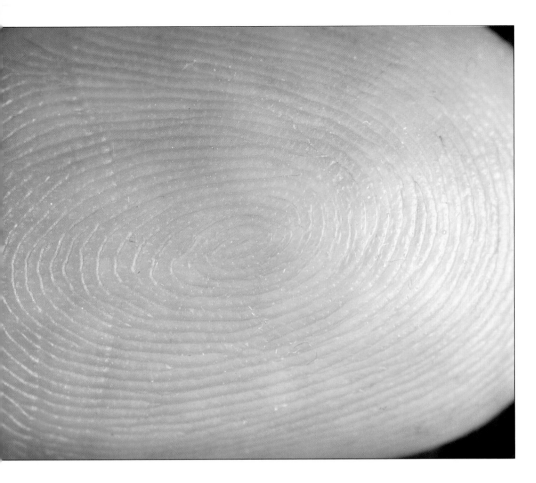

The pattern on this person's fingertip is unique and will help distinguish him or her from millions of other people.

Farther down, in the lower levels of the skin and in the joints, tendons, and muscles are nerve endings that respond to stronger stimuli—a book in your hand, a pat on your back, the pressure of your foot on the floor. These are called pressure receptors. They, too, send messages to the brain via the spinal cord. But they will not respond to the feather, the draft, or the drop of water.

We all need both types of receptor—touch and pressure—to enable us to register what is going on around us and to react in the right way. If you touch something hot, you need to be able to pull away quickly. But you wouldn't want to react in the same way to a warm summer breeze on your face.

Some parts of the body have more touch receptors than others. For example, the tip of your tongue can distinguish between two different stimuli that are only a fraction of an inch apart on its surface. Your back is much less sensitive and the stimuli would need to be a couple of inches apart before the touch receptors could distinguish between them.

You have one more specialized type of touch receptor, called a muscle spindle. These are found in the muscles and they act as stretch receptors to tell you when your muscles are relaxed and to tell you when your muscles need to contract so that you can move.

FINGERPRINTS

The tips of your fingers need to be very sensitive because you use them to do most of your touching. The pattern of skin on your fingertips is unique. It is called your fingerprint and it is different from everyone else's. If you turn to a life of crime, the police will become very interested in your fingerprints. If you touch a smooth surface at the scene of your crime, you will leave the pattern of your fingerprints behind and the police will have proof that you've been there.

THE SKIN

The dark-skinned children in this picture will not suffer sunburn as badly as the fair-skinned boy.

The skin isn't just a home for touch receptors. It has four other essential jobs. First, it protects all the internal parts of the body from damage. Cells in the top layer of the epidermis, called the *stratum corneum*, contain a protein called keratin, which makes the skin waterproof. The more keratin that cells contain, the tougher they become, until they are just hard, dead cells that eventually rub away. Some parts of the body, such as the soles of the feet, have a much thicker *stratum corneum* than others. This is so they can stand up to a lot of wear and tear.

The skin's second job is to regulate body temperature. It does this in several ways. The most obvious way is by release of sweat from tiny pores in the surface of the skin when body temperature goes above 98.6°F. As sweat evaporates, temperature goes down.

When you are hot, you don't just sweat, you go red. This is because blood vessels in the dermis—the layer below the epidermis—have gotten wider to let more blood go through your skin so that the air can cool it down. When you are cold, all the blood vessels in your skin get narrower so less blood comes to the surface. You stay warmer when less of your blood is exposed to the cold air on your skin.

Indirectly, your skin helps keep you warm by providing a storehouse for fat. Fat is deposited in the lower parts of the dermis and under the skin. It acts as insulation against the cold.

The skin's last job is quite different. It's the factory for Vitamin D production in your body. You need Vitamin D for strong bones and you get some of it from your food. But in the skin, Vitamin D is made from a type of steroid called a sterol. When you go outside, the sterols are converted into Vitamin D by the sunlight.

SHEDDING YOUR SKIN

You shed your epidermis every thirty days. Cells are made in the lower part of the epidermis and gradually move to the surface, where they become increasingly keratinized, die, and are shed. In some people, such as those with a skin disease called psoriasis, this process is too fast. It takes only five days from birth to death of cells. This makes the surface of their skin scaly and itchy.

This person has psoriasis on her hands. You can see the painful pink scaly marks that mean her skin cells are being shed too fast.

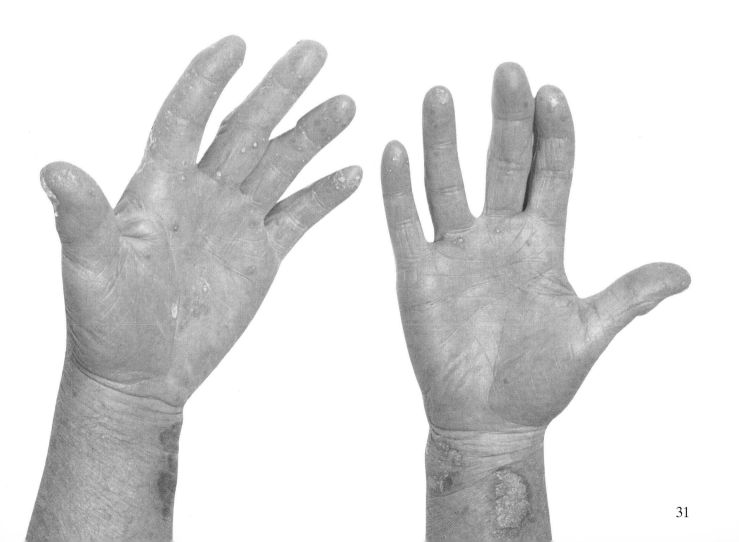

HAIR AND NAILS

Humans have hair and nails; other mammals have claws, hooves, horns, and antlers; reptiles have scales; and birds have feathers. They are all different forms of *stratum corneum*.

Hair and nails grow from the root—from the hair follicle embedded in the scalp and from the nail bed embedded in the skin. The cells nearest the follicle or the nail bed get oxygen and nutrients from blood vessels nearby. But as the cells in the follicle divide, older cells move up the shaft of the hair or along the nail and lose their blood supply. The cells gradually fill up with keratin and die.

How soon your skin, hair, and nail cells die will depend on how well you look after them. Dryness is the big enemy! The drier your skin, your hair, or your nails, the faster the dead and dying cells will fall off.

Washing a lot won't keep them moist. It will wash away the natural oils that keep your hair, skin, and nails from becoming dry. Water will also soften your nails and make them split.

Cutting them into a pointed shape will make them prone to breaking, too—a rounded or square shape will make them stronger.

You should try not to wash your hair more than two or three times a week. But if it seems to be very greasy and you feel you must wash it more often, choose a mild shampoo that won't strip away the natural oils. If you dye or perm your hair, you'll have to be especially careful. You should always test the chemicals on a lock of your hair to see how it reacts before you treat all your hair.

The chemicals in hair dyes and perming lotions damage the hair. So you should use shampoos and conditioners specially designed to reduce the damage done by chemicals.

Hair and nails can become diseased. Nails may become infected, but they can be treated with antibiotics or antifungal drugs. Fungi can also attack the scalp so patches of hair fall out. This can be treated with drugs. Other types of hair loss are much harder to treat.

Nail polish can help protect nails from splits and breaks caused by a lot of washing.

Dark hair tends to shine more than blond hair. But the secret of healthy hair lies in using gentle shampoos and steering clear of harsh dyes and perms.

WILL I GO BALD?

About 40 percent of men lose some of their hair by the time they are thirty-five and 60 percent by the age of sixty. And there isn't much they can do about it. Most cases are due to male pattern baldness, which runs in families. If your mother's father is bald, there's a good chance you will be, too. Hair recedes from the forehead or thinning starts on the crown and gradually spreads over most of the head.

TOUCH ME, HEAL ME

This baby knows it is safe. It can feel its mother and knows she will protect it from danger.

Touching makes us feel safe and feel cared for. From the moment we are born, touch binds us to those around us. Watch any young animal investigating its surroundings. At the first sign of trouble, it runs back to its mother for reassurance. Knowing she is there—either by seeing or hearing her—isn't enough. Tiger cub, fawn, calf, or puppy, it needs to touch its mother and feel her caring response. A human baby cannot run to its mother. But it learns very quickly that if it opens its mouth and howls, someone will come and pick it up and hold it.

As they get older, some people use touch to convey their emotions more than others. Some families are more "huggy" than others. Children who don't get a lot of hugs and kisses are less likely to touch other people, and they, in turn, will probably not do a lot of hugging and kissing when they have children.

In general, men probably find it harder to express their emotions through touch than women. While many women will greet a close friend of either sex with a kiss and a hug, men are more likely to shake hands, particularly with someone of the same sex.

When did you last allow your mother or sister to kiss you in public? From the age of eight or nine until they are about eighteen or twenty, most boys are appalled if their mother or sister kisses them in public. But a girl probably wouldn't think twice about kissing her family in front of her friends.

It's nice to use touch to show that you care about people, but it can also be very intrusive. We all have to learn what behavior is acceptable to other people and what isn't. People who rarely express their emotions through touch may be deeply embarrassed if you grab them in a bear hug! Others may be deeply hurt if you turn away when they reach toward you.

TOUCH THERAPY

Autistic children are very withdrawn. They don't touch or like to be touched but prefer to live in a world of their own and not play with other children. Part of the treatment to help them come out of themselves includes a lot of hugging and cuddling.

Friends? A touch of the hands tells these two teenagers that all is well between them. There's no need to fight.

PAINFUL TOUCH

In 1985, 663,000 people in the United States were treated in the hospital for burns. A great number of them were children. Boiling kettles, pans on stoves, and flammable liquids, like gas and paint thinner are often to blame for burn accidents. About 90 percent of people do now survive their burns. But despite remarkable advances in surgery, many people are left with terrible scars. Prevention is definitely better than cure.

Burns are classified "superficial," "deep dermal," and "full thickness." Superficial burns affect only the outer layer of the skin and generally heal on their own. Deep dermal burns penetrate into the lower skin layer. They usually need a skin graft but can heal very well. Full thickness burns go right through the skin to the tissue underneath and, even with a skin graft, will leave a scar.

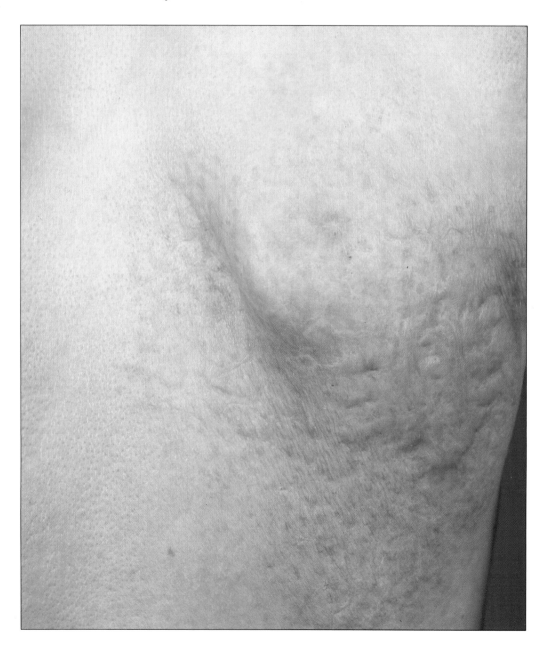

This skin graft is almost as good as new. The new cells have joined with the surrounding area and get oxygen and nutrients from blood vessels nearby.

IF YOU BURN YOURSELF . . .

Put the burned area in cold water right away. This will relieve the pain and help prevent the burn from going any deeper. Try to remove clothing or anything covering the burn, especially if it is still smoldering. Don't put any creams or ointments on the burn. Get help immediately.

When someone arrives at a hospital with bad burns, the main worry is dehydration. Burns ooze huge amounts of fluid and this can lead to death, often several days after the injury.

The next big worry is infection. Burns are an easy target for every passing germ and people who are badly burned cannot defend themselves against attack. So they will probably need a lot of antibiotics.

As soon as the patient is well enough, the surgeons decide what surgery is needed. If they wait too long, the tissue around muscles and joints may become permanently damaged so movement becomes very difficult.

Skin grafting means taking a piece of healthy skin and putting it over a burn. A thin layer of cells is removed and stretched to about four to six times its original size. This is laid on the burned area so that new cells can grow up through the mesh part of the graft.

Sometimes thicker grafts have to be used. These leave a scar on the part of the body from which the graft is taken, such as the thigh. But this may be better than leaving a scar in a much more visible area, such as the face. Another option is to stretch the skin near the burn so that it covers the damaged area.

ICY TOUCH

Do your fingers ever feel so cold that they turn blue-white and numb? Your body is trying to warm you up by stopping the blood from going to your limbs where it will cool down. It's also a warning that you need to dress more warmly. It's better to wear several layers of light clothes than a single thick layer. This is because clothes act as insulation and trap air. Heavy, thick clothes will push the air out and reduce insulation.

It doesn't matter if the blood supply to your fingers and toes is reduced for a short time, although it may hurt a bit when the blood rushes back. But if the blood supply is cut off for very long, cells in the fingers and toes start to die. This is what happens when mountaineers get frostbite. If they can't get warm, their fingers and toes are irreparably damaged and may even drop off or have to be amputated.

Elderly people who don't move around very much are at risk from getting too cold. Every winter some die of hypothermia. This means their whole body temperature drops from a normal of around 98.6°F to only 95°F. It may not sound like much, but those few degrees can mean the difference between life and death. As body temperature falls, organs, such as the heart,

Always be sure you are warmly dressed when you go out in the cold.

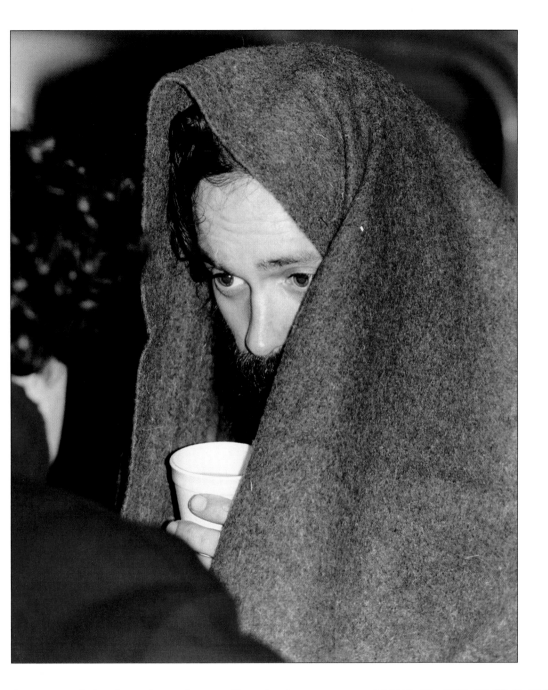

Many homeless people risk hypothermia when sleeping outside in cold weather. The lucky ones receive blankets and hot drinks from charity workers.

lungs, and brain, slow down. People become confused and don't realize they need to get warm again. In the end, they become unconscious and they may die.

Some people suffer from a condition called Raynaud's syndrome. The small blood vessels in their fingers and toes become extra-sensitive to the cold. They suddenly get narrower so less blood can get through. Their fingers and toes become white and are very cold. Raynaud's syndrome sufferers should be especially careful to keep their hands and feet warm and dry.

WARMING UP

People who are suffering from the effects of extreme cold need to be treated with care. They need to warm up slowly, so don't put them right in front of a hot fire or cover them with hot-water bottles. Instead, move them into a warmer room and turn the heat up. Take off any wet clothes, wrap them in warm blankets, and give them warm drinks like hot chocolate—not alcoholic drinks. If this doesn't work, call a doctor.

LOOKING AFTER YOUR SKIN

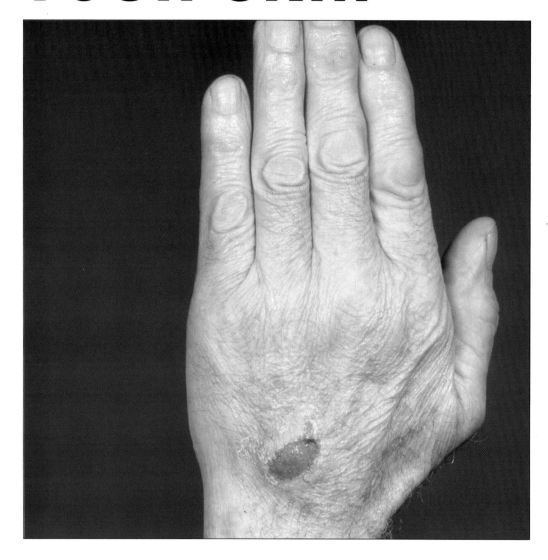

Lengthy exposure to strong sunlight is a major cause of skin cancers such as this sebaceous cell carcinoma.

You're never too young to start looking after your skin. You may not think you are doing any harm by lying in the sun, lounging in a hot bath, or getting chemicals on it. But in twenty years' time you'll reap the reward of your carelessness! Dry, wrinkled, leathery skin, with all its natural elasticity gone for good, is not a pretty sight!

The sun is public enemy number one to your skin. Pale, white skins are simply not made to withstand a hot Mediterranean sun. The skin gets its color from a pigment called melanin. Fair-skinned people have much smaller quantities of melanin in their skin than brown- or black-skinned people. Sunlight stimulates skin cells called melanocytes to make more melanin and produce a tan. But, in doing so, it also causes a lot of damage.

Sunlight contains two main types of rays—ultraviolet A (UV-A) and ultraviolet B (UV-B). Until recently scientists thought that only UV-B was harmful. UV-B burns the skin and it attacks the genetic material in skin cells and turns them cancerous. In the last decade there has been a big increase in the number of cases of skin cancer, especially the most dangerous type, malignant melanoma. This coincides with the big increase in numbers of people spending more and more time in the sun.

Scientists now know that UV-A can also be dangerous. It makes the skin age faster than normal so that it becomes lined and wrinkled. This is especially worrisome for people who lie under sunlamps, since these use UV-A to produce a so-called suntan.

The best idea is to stay out of the sun or to cover up when you are out of doors. Today's top fashion models have already learned that lesson. They don't risk their skin in the sun. Most keep to their natural skin color. And if they do sport a suntan, you can be pretty sure it has come out of a bottle, not from hours on a beach!

SLIP, SLAP, SLOP

"Slip on a T-shirt, slap on a hat, slop on some sunscreen" goes the advice to Australian sun worshipers. Everyone should use a sunscreen when they go out in the sun. Be sure it protects against UV-A as well as UV-B rays. Fair-skinned people should use a sunscreen with a protection factor of at least fifteen, and darker-skinned people who don't burn as easily should use at least factor eight.

Always build up the time you spend in the sun gradually. Don't go and lie out for twelve hours on the first day or you'll be lobster-pink and very sore for the rest of your vacation. Always use a moisturizer after you have sunbathed to help put back some of the moisture you have taken out lying in the sun.

It's better to be safe than sorry. Sunscreens protect against the ravages of the sun. If you burn your skin, you'll be more likely to get skin cancer and your skin will age quickly.

TURNING BACK THE CLOCK

If you pinch the skin on the back of your hand, it will immediately bounce back into shape when you let go. Do that to the skin of someone twenty years older than you and it will take longer. Do it to someone in their eighties and the skin won't spring back; it will stay pinched-looking until you flatten it out with your hand.

Each year thousands of people spend millions of dollars on creams, cosmetics, and plastic surgery in an attempt to turn back the clock on their aging skin. Are they wasting their money? Surgeons can do far more for aging skin than they could twenty years ago. But they can't work miracles. Even well-looked-after skin loses some of its elasticity as it gets older.

Skin ages deep down in the dermis, which is crisscrossed with coils of tough fibers made from a protein called collagen and fine elastic fibers made from a protein called elastin. These expand and contract as the skin stretches and relaxes. Together, they give the skin its strength and flexibility. As skin ages, the collagen fibers lose their shape and the elastic fibers lose their elasticity. The dermis becomes thinner and drier.

So what does aging skin need to give it back its bounce? Water? New collagen and elastic fibers? Moisturizing creams are supposed to put some fluid back into the skin. But you rub them onto the dead and dying epidermis of the skin, not the dermis where the real trouble lies.

As you get older, your skin gradually becomes drier and thinner. In time, it loses much of its elasticity and you develop wrinkles.

A few lines give character to a face. A facelift might get rid of some of the wrinkles, but it wouldn't last forever. In a few years her skin would sag again.

Some manufacturers have developed creams that, they claim, can get down to the dermis. These creams contain moisturizers wrapped up in fatty envelopes called liposomes. In theory, the liposomes get through the epidermis to the dermis. But no one really knows what happens to them when they get there.

Some people have small amounts of collagen injected under their skin to try to give it bounce. Some models and movie stars have the injections in their lips to make them fuller. Unfortunately, the collagen soon breaks down and within a few weeks or months their skin sags as much as ever.

The only other option is to pull the sagging skin taut. This is what a facelift does. The skin is cut away from the face all around the hairline and any unwanted fat is sucked out from underneath. The skin is then pulled taut and stitched back into place. If it is done well, the only clue is that the person suddenly looks ten or twenty years younger. If it is done badly, their face will be pulled into a permanent smile! Either way, it won't last forever.

STRIPPING OFF

People with fine laughter lines around their eyes and mouths can have a chemical peel. A special chemical is painted on the skin and left to burn away the top layer of cells. The skin is very red and sore for a few days. But when it heals, fine lines will have disappeared. Deeper lines and wrinkles can't be removed this way.

SIXTH SENSE

Sight, hearing, smell, taste, and touch. These are the five senses we know about and understand. But some people believe they have a sixth sense. They can "see" the future or they "know" what other people are thinking.

We've all experienced some of these things. We call a friend and find they were trying to phone us. We say the same thing as someone else, at exactly the same time. We get a feeling that we've been somewhere before, although we know we haven't.

Is it just coincidence? Or do we have some special sixth sense that we don't yet understand? There are large sections of our brains that have no obvious function. Perhaps they control senses that we just don't realize that we have. If we don't realize them, why do we have them?

A sixth sense may be too much to ask for. But some people do seem to have more insight into what people are thinking than others, and it helps them make decisions. Others seem to be rather "thick-skinned." They don't realize what people are thinking and they say and do things that upset people. They don't really watch the expression on people's faces or listen to what they are saying—and what they are not saying. They don't make the most of all the information that they are receiving from their senses. They don't realize just how powerful their five senses can be.

LEFT Uri Geller—a man famous for bending spoons by sheer willpower. Is it a con, or is he really psychic?

RIGHT Look at the expression on this girl's face and analyze her body language. Can you tell how she is feeling? Are you using your sixth sense?

GLOSSARY

addiction physical or mental craving for a substance.

anesthetic drug that prevents a person from feeling pain.

antibiotics drugs that kill bacteria.

anticoagulant drug that makes the blood thinner so that it does not clot so easily.

aromatherapy use of strong-smelling oils to improve mood and physical well-being.

carnivore meat-eating animal.

chocoholic person with a strong craving for chocolate.

collagen protein found in fibers below the skin that gives the skin its strength.

dehydration too little water in the body.

dermis lower layer of the skin.

elastin protein found in fibers beneath the skin that gives the skin its elasticity.

epidermis outer layer of the skin.

genetic material DNA in all cells that helps to determine a person's character and looks.

hypothermia dangerous condition when body temperature drops to 95°F or below.

keratin protein that makes the skin waterproof.

malignant melanoma serious form of skin cancer.

omnivore animal that eats both meat and plants.

pheromone chemical substance used as a sexual attractant to communicate with another member of the same species.

prototype new type of product before it is fully tested and mass-produced.

Raynaud's syndrome medical condition that makes the blood vessels in the fingers and toes get smaller and constrict the blood flow.

receptor nerve endings that recognize pressure on the skin.

steroids group of chemicals found throughout the body and used, among other things, to make some hormones.

FURTHER READING

Edelson, Edward. *Aging.* New York:
Chelsea House, 1991.

Kittredge, Mary. *The Human Body: An Overview.* New York: Chelsea House, 1990.

Novick, Nelson L. *Skin Care for Teens.* New York: Franklin Watts, 1988.

Parker, Steve. *The Body and How It Works.* New York: Dorling Kindersley, 1992.

Silverstein, Alvin et al. *Overcoming Acne: The How and Why of Healthy Skin Care.* New York: Morrow Junior Books, 1992.

———. *Smell, the Subtle Sense.* New York: Morrow Junior Books, 1992.

Time-Life Book Editors. *The Human Body.* Alexandria, Virginia: Time-Warner Books, 1989.

ACKNOWLEDGMENTS

Life Science Images 31; Oxford Scientific Films 11 (G. Bernard), 29 (G. Bernard); Reflections cover and title page, 22; Rex 8 (Paul Brown), 14, 18, 27, 35, 44 (S. Clarke); Robert Harding 12 (top, P. Arnold), 26 (G. White) Science Photo Library 4 (Dr. J. Burgess), 7 (Prof. P. Motta), 10 (top, David Campione), 13 (Damien Lovegrove), 23 (St. Bartholomew's Hospital), 28 (Gene Cox), 36 (James Stevenson), 40 (James Stevenson), 41 (Shiela Terry); Skjold 30, 38, 45; Tony Stone Worldwide 5 (Dan Bosler), 6 (James Jackson), 9 (John Moss), 12 (bottom, Barbara Filet), 17 (David Sutherland), 19 (James Jackson), 21 (Stephen Studd), 24, 33 (top, Mark Lewis), 34 (Johan Elzenga), 43 (Dale Durfee); Topham 15, 25, 32, 39; WPL 33 (bottom), 37, 42; Zefa 10 (bottom), 16.

INDEX